BACH
FOR UNACCOMPANIED FLUTE

These arrangements of movements from the sonatas and partitas and suites of J. S. Bach are intended for private study rather than for public performance. Although they were not originally written as flute music it should be remembered that Bach's instrumental writing was of a universal nature: he himself considered his music transferable to any instrument, wind, string or keyboard, whose compass it happened to fit. When it did not fit he never hesitated to transpose or rearrange.

Flautists, however advanced, will find the pieces bristling with problems of phrasing, articulation and breath control and, it need hardly be said, musically more rewarding than the studies specially composed by the flute virtuosi of the past. They may also be found useful as studies of endurance in preparation for the composer's flute sonatas — possibly the most exhausting works in the flautist's repertoire. Care should be taken, however, to avoid tiring the embouchure: it is better to stop at a double bar or any convenient full close than to risk possible harm to the tone production or intonation by persevering with a tired lip.

The phrasing and dynamic marks are only suggestions and no attempt has been made to indicate where breath should be taken. These problems, as well as the very wide choice of tempi, are interdependent and their many possible solutions should be considered part of the player's study. Tempo indications in brackets are editorial.

No. 2 is from Sonata No. 1 (violin); Nos. 5, 7, and 9 from Suite No. 1 (cello); Nos. 3, 10, and 15 from Suite No. 2 (cello); Nos. 8 and 14 from Suite No. 3 (cello); No. 11 and 17 from Suite No. 4 (cello); No. 6 from Suite No. 5 (cello); Nos. 13 and 16 from Partita No. 1 (violin); No. 12 from Partita No. 2 (violin); Nos. 1 and 4 from Partita No. 3 (violin).

F.S.

BACH
FÜR QUERFLÖTE OHNE BEGLEITUNG

Diese Bearbeitungen einiger Sätze aus den Sonaten, Partiten und Suiten J. S. Bachs sind mehr für das private Üben als für öffentliche Aufführungen bestimmt. Obwohl sie ursprünglich nicht als Flötenmusik geschrieben wurden, sollte man bedenken, daß Bachs Instrumentalwerk von allumfassendem Charakter war: Er selbst betrachtete seine Musik als übertragbar auf jedes Instrument, dessen Stimmumfang sie gerade entsprach-Blas-, Streich- oder Tasteninstrument. Wenn sie ihm nicht entsprach, zögerte er niemals zu transponieren oder neu zu setzen.

Flötisten, wie fortgeschritten sie auch sein mögen, werden feststellen, daß die Stücke voller Schwierigkeiten stecken, was Phrasierung, Artikulation und Atemkontrolle betrifft. Es braucht dabei kaum erwähnt zu werden, daß sie musikalisch lohnender sind als die Etüden, die von den Flötenvirtuosen der Vergangenheit besonders für Übungszwecke komponiert wurden. Man wird sie vielleicht auch nützlich finden als Übungen im Aushalten als Vorbereitung auf die Flötensonaten des Komponisten—möglicherweise die anstrengendsten Werke im Repertoire eines Flötisten. Man sollte jedoch darauf achten, den Ansatz nicht zu stark zu beanspruchen: Es ist besser, an einem doppelten Taktstrich oder irgend einem passenden Abschluß aufzuhören, als mit ermüdeter Lippe weiterzuspielen und dabei vielleicht der Tonerzeugung und Intonation zu schaden.

Die Phrasierung und die dynamischen Zeichen sind nur Vorschläge, und wir haben keinen Versuch gemacht anzudeuten, wo Atem geholt werden sollte. Diese Probleme, sowie auch die sehr weitgehende Auswahl der Tempi, greifen ineinander über, und ihre vielen möglichen Lösungen sollten für den Spieler als ein Teil seiner Studien gelten. Die Tempo Hinweise in Klammern stammen vom Herausgeber.

Nr. 2 ist aus der Sonate Nr. 1 (Violine); Nrn. 5, 7 und 9 aus der Suite Nr. 1 (Violoncello); Nrn. 3, 10 und 15 aus der Suite Nr. 2 (Violoncello); Nrn. 8 und 14 aus der Suite Nr. 3 (Violoncello); Nrn. 11 und 17 aus der Suite Nr. 4 (Violoncello); Nr. 6 aus der Suite Nr. 5 (Violoncello); Nrn. 13 und 16 aus der Partita Nr. 1 (Violine); Nr. 12 aus der Partita Nr. 2 (Violine); Nrn. 1 und 4 aus der Partita Nr. 3 (Violine).

F.S.

BACH
FOR UNACCOMPANIED FLUTE

arranged by Fritz Spiegl

1. GIGUE

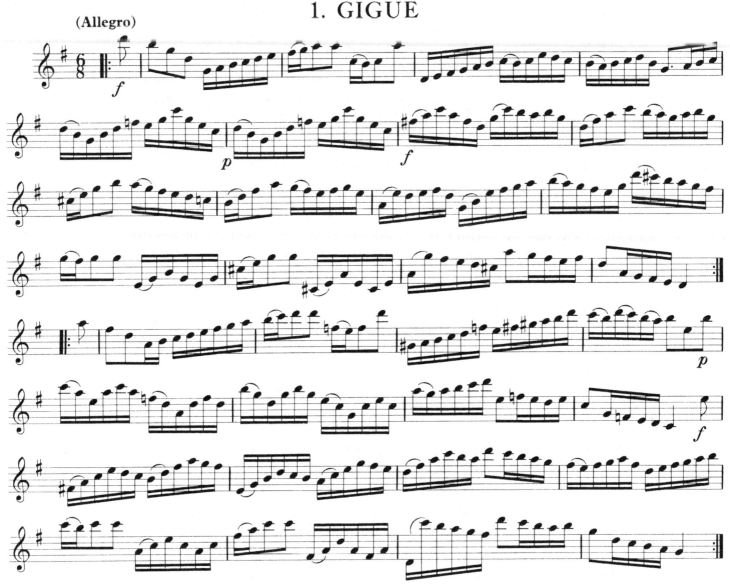

The semiquavers may also be practised *legato* or tongued throughout.

2. PRELUDE

Printed in Great Britain
OXFORD UNIVERSITY PRESS, MUSIC DEPARTMENT, GREAT CLARENDON STREET, OXFORD OX2 6DP

The semiquavers may also be played

3. SARABANDE

★ Trills should begin on the upper note.

Bach for unaccompanied flute

4

4. BOURRÉE

5. ALLEMANDE

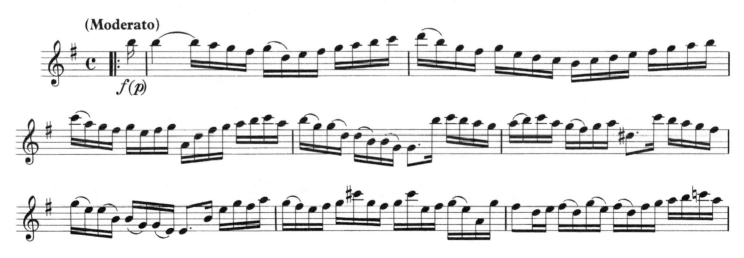

Bach for unaccompanied flute

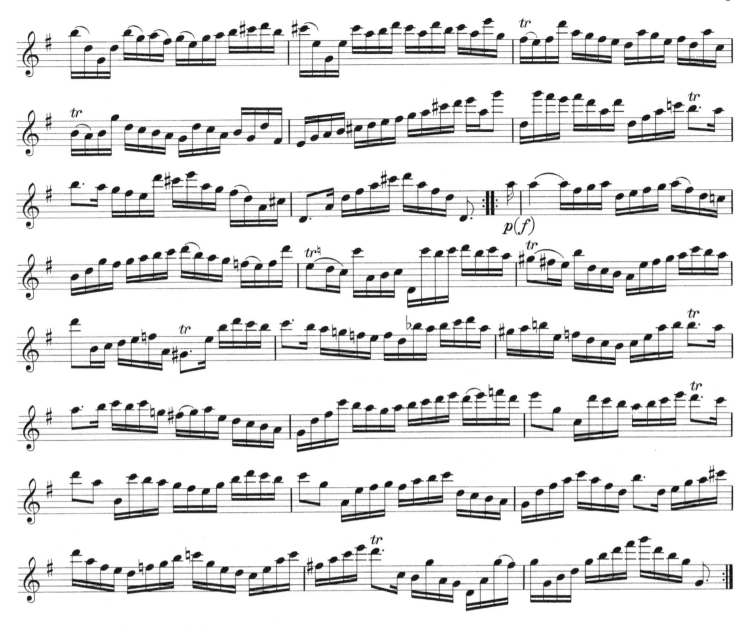

6. SARABANDE

7. COURANTE

8. TWO BOURRÉES

8

9. GIGUE

May also be played tongued throughout

10. MINUET

Bach for unaccompanied flute

11. BOURRÉE

Alternative phrasing for the predominant figures in this piece:

Bach for unaccompanied flute

12. ALLEMANDE

13. DOUBLE

This movement may also be played *legato/pianissimo* throughout.

Bach for unaccompanied flute

14. GIGUE

★ to ★ may also be practised

15. COURANTE

★ Flautists who possess an instrument with a low B may prefer to play the last five notes an octave lower.

Bach for unaccompanied flute

16. DOUBLE

Bach for unaccompanied flute

Bach for unaccompanied flute

17. GIGUE

Alternative phrasings ♩♩♩ or ♩♩♩ may be applied throughout.

Bach for unaccompanied flute

Processed and printed by
Halstan & Co. Ltd., Amersham, Bucks., England

OXFORD UNIVERSITY PRESS